WHY THEY KNEEL

A Kids Guidebook To The African American History Museum

By Kyra Bush & Christian Sarem

AuthorHouse™
1663 Liberty Drive
Bloomington, IN 47403
www.authorhouse.com
Phone: 833-262-8899

Because of the dynamic nature of the Internet, any web addresses or links contained in this book may have changed since publication and may no longer be valid. The views expressed in this work are solely those of the author and do not necessarily reflect the views of the publisher, and the publisher hereby disclaims any responsibility for them.

Any people depicted in stock imagery provided by Getty Images are models, and such images are being used for illustrative purposes only. Certain stock imagery © Getty Images.

This book is printed on acid-free paper.

ISBN: 978-1-6655-2514-5 (sc)
ISBN: 978-1-6655-2513-8 (e)

Library of Congress Control Number: 2021909401

Print information available on the last page.

Published by AuthorHouse 05/06/2021

authorHOUSE®

DEDICATION

This book is dedicated to our father and grandfather, Charles V. Bush. The first African American Supreme Court Page, and first African American graduate of the Air Force Academy. He helped to desegregate our great American institutions and was a leader and inspiration to us all.

ACKNOWLEDGMENTS

Thank you to the Smithsonian National African American History Museum for acknowledging the accomplishments of Charles V. Bush and including him in the museum. Our family is honored to be a part of your magnificent tribute to our culture.

Thank you to the Wilcox Agency for your guidance and direction, in turning our vision into reality.

TABLE OF CONTENTS

INTRODUCTION

"Why does Colin Kaepernick take a knee during the National Anthem?", my little brother asked me while we were watching Sunday night football. I thought about all of the new reports of police brutality toward African American men and women arising through cities across the United States, and all of the protests against it.

But, I also thought of the pictures I had seen of Olympic Athletes in the 1960's wearing black arm bands and raising their fists in similar protest. It seemed as though peaceful protest had a long history in our country, and it was time for him to learn about it.

Our nation has a history of segregation and inequality toward African Americans and achieving equality has been a long and difficult struggle. Martin Luther King Jr., John Lewis, Rosa Parks many other remarkable leaders fought to get us where we are today, but we still have a long way to go. Our country's founders dreamed of our country forming "a more perfect union", and the only way we can get there is by citizens of all colors being equal, and through peaceful protest, or what John Lewis called getting in "good trouble". The dream and goal of all citizens should be that we might see "a more perfect union" in our lifetime.

The First Colonel An original sepia-toned image depicts Cadet Charles Young upon graduating from the U.S. Military Academy in 1889. Young became the first Regular Army African American colonel.

Court-Martial Orders These General Court-Martial Orders No. 39 discharged Lt. Henry Flipper from the Army in 1882. In 1999 Flipper was cleared and posthumously re-awarded his commission.

West Point Register Cadet Johnson Chestnut Whittaker, listed in this register, was an African American discharged from West Point after four years in 1880 amid suspicious circumstances still debated by historians.

Jesse Wrice's Mess Dress Uniform Jacket Jesse E. Wrice, who chose to join the Marine Corps, graduated from the Naval Academy more than 30 years after Wesley Brown became the first African American graduate in 1949. Gift of Jesse E. Wrice Jr.

Gold Star Mother Medal This Gold Star Mother Medal was given to Colonel Benjamin O. Davis for his service as the official escort to African American Gold Star Mothers. On loan from U.S. Army Heritage and Education Center.

James McCullin's Purple Heart McCullin deprived on April... shot down on July 2,... birthday. McCullin's... Peggy's birthday.

demies

...ve high...rition rates. Until ...ostra... nd discrimination ... Africa...ericans. During ...an Ame...who attended ...d. The al...n ratio ...y. The f...w African ...ce academ...broke through ...e the early ...ersonal co...ity programs, ...tablished ...n in 1976.

Air Force Academy In 1963 Charles V. Bush became the first African American graduate of the Air Force Academy. An intelligence officer, he served in Vietnam and spoke Vietnamese fluently. U.S. Air Force Academy

First Class of Women In 1980 Gail Benjamin Colvin graduated in the first class of women at the Air Force Academy. She retired as a colonel in 2010 after 30 years of service. U.S. Air Force Academy

Gold

After W... the w... Mo...

turn me 'ro...

PROLOGUE

We walked into the museum, excited and eager to find the tribute to my grandfather. The museum was busy, and had escalators going downstairs, and also leading at least two floors upstairs. My mom grabbed my hand and gazed down at me, **"I know we want to go straight to where your grandfather is, but lets do this right"**, she studied the pamphlet they handed out at the door.

"Lets start at the bottom floor of the museum, because I think everything that led up to the moment where your grandfather has his special place in history will explain how he got there. We need to understand how he got to that moment in time, and all of the stories of others that brought him there." I was frustrated, but I understood the importance of hearing others stories, because their moments in time build upon each other and bring us to where we are now, so I followed as she led us to the escalator. We start at the bottom and rise up through history, to make sense of the present and embrace the future.

U.S. BRIG PERRY,　　　　　　　　　　　　　AMERICAN SLAVE SHIP MARTHA.

"off Ambriz June 6th 1850"

HISTORY GALLERIES C3- SLAVERY AND FREEDOM

1400-1877

My mom led me down the escalator stairs to the history galleries. There was so much to see, so we followed the path. It began with the TransAtlantic slave trade, where we learned about the Africans that were torn from their homeland by the Europeans, and sold into slavery. They were then brought to America by boat, against their will and forced to work on the land of the slave owners. They were treated as the property of their slave owners, without any rights. We learned that the slaves were recruited to fight in the Revolutionary War to fight for American Independence from the British. We got to see an actual slave cabin, and what it may have

looked like during that time, and learned about their daily life and work, most having worked in tobacco and cotton fields. From there we saw exhibits about the civil war, and the fight to free the slaves, which eventually happened in 1856.

C2-DEFENDING FREEDOM, DEFINING FREEDOM

Era of Segregation 1876-1968

As we walked further down the path, we saw a huge bus in the middle of the room, and a line of people that extended around the corner! The bus was a replica of an actual segregated rail car from that era! We got to board the bus and see the inside of what buses looked like back then! There were separate places to sit for white people and "colored' people.

I couldn't help but think about Rosa Parks on a similar bus, tired, feet aching from working all day, sitting in the front of the bus, and refusing to give up her seat. One of the first peaceful protests of the Jim Crow era. Across from the bus was an interactive lunch counter, where you could guess questions about what African American experiences were during that time. Were they allowed to just walk in and sit down in any diner? Were they allowed to sit wherever they wanted? Could they drink out of any water fountain or did they have to go to a different one?

This led us to learning more about the Jim Crow laws, and how they were created to keep "separate but equal" living conditions for African Americans. Jim Crow laws forced African Americans to have separate schools, water fountains, stores, diners, and even places to sit on a bus- whites in front, "coloreds" in back. All of this to prevent the co-mingling of the different ethnicities, because of fear and hatred.

I still wondered what that long line was for, and discovered it was the line to see the Emmet Till memorial. Emmet Till was significant to African Americans because he is a symbol for African Americans throughout history being unjustly prosecuted for crimes they did not commit and not always getting a fair day in court, as promised to them under the law. This is what happened to Emmet Till.

Although slavery had ended, African Americans were still being jailed and killed by police at an alarming rate. In fact, the police force was originally formed to patrol for escaped slaves. Slavery was replaced with prisons for many African American men. From what I could tell, our country still had a long way to go during that time before people were no longer judged by the color of their skin.

Modern Civil Rights Movement

The Great Migration came next, which was the movement of six million African Americans out of the South, where most had known slavery in their lifetime, to the Northeast, Midwest and West which were known to be less hostile to African Americans. With the Great Migration came better education, opportunities and wealth for those that chose to leave the South. The former slaves began to leave plantations and farms between 1916 and 1970 in search of a better life.

As we headed up the ramp toward the next floor, in front of us was a replica of an airplane! I knew right away it was one flown by the Tuskegee airmen, who were notorious for being the first African American airmen to serve in a war. They were known for their service in World War 2 and for their heroism, and courage in serving their country that did not always treat

them well. I knew about them because my grandfather served in the air force and to see it up close and in person was impressive!

C1 CHANGING AMERICA: 1968 and beyond

Next came the Events of '68, where there was so much to see, because it was such a definitive moment in history. Martin Luther King Jr. led a revolution of people to fight for equal rights, regardless of skin color, and encouraged peaceful protest. He was well known for his "I have a dream" speech, and for his words uplifting and empowering a generation. When Colin Kaepernick took a knee during the American Anthem during a football game it was to protest the way African Americans are treated by law enforcement. We still see Americans peacefully protesting today, when players take a knee, lock arms, or hold hands during the American Anthem at sporting events, as part of a peaceful protest against unequal treatment for African Americans that still exists today. The Black Panthers and Malcolm X promoted a more hostile approach to change and believed extreme non peaceful actions were necessary to make significant change in our country. It was eye opening to see pictures and video of the protests and marches that were so important to the civil rights movement and compare them to the Black Lives Matter protests and marches we have been a part of in 2020.

The Movement Marches On

Cities and Suburbs

Part of the civil rights movement was the migration of African Americans to the suburbs of the East, North, Midwest, and West, in search of a better education for their children. An important part of this movement was the court ruling of Brown v Board of Education which decided that African American children had a right to an equal education as white children, so they were gradually integrated into white schools, which a lot of schools and towns resisted. Some people were so angry that they protested in front of the schools not to let African American children in, and some of the kids had to be escorted into the schools by police, all while people yelled hateful words at them. As part of this decision, my grandfather was selected to be the first African American Supreme Court Page. This meant he interacted with the Justices on the Supreme Court, and was part of all of the traditions our country holds dear. He was thirteen when he was chosen, the same age as me, and he was already making a difference in our country!

Decades

As we made our way through the museum, we were excited to see the exhibit for Barack Obama! One of my earliest memories is sitting with my brother studying a placemat of The Presidents of the USA. We knew every single one. We also noticed that none of them looked quite like we did. Was it really true that any kid could grow up to be President? **Then came Barack Obama.** The 2008 election was an exciting time for my family. My parents, grandparents, cousins, aunts and uncles were all anxious for the results of such a historical election. My grandfather always believed that he would see an African American president in his lifetime. Back when he was a boy, he even held onto the hope that one day it might be him. For me and my brother, the election of Obama meant that one day, if we chose, we could have the opportunity to become President too!

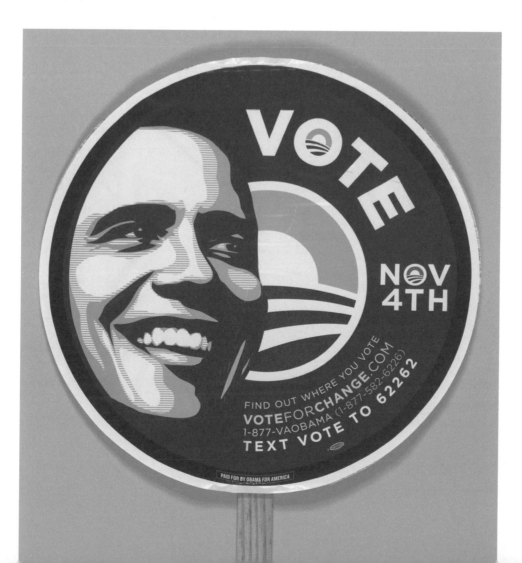

WATERFALL-CONCOURSE

As we walked up the ramp to the next floor, we could hear the rushing water before we could see it. As we entered the room it looked like it was raining in a sheet coming straight from the ceiling. I had never seen anything like it, so we sat on a bench and just watched and listened as the water came down. On the walls were famous quotes, "I cherish my own freedom dearly, but I care even more for your freedom," reads a 1991 quote from South African leader Nelson Mandela.

*"I ask no monument, proud and high to arrest
the gaze of the passers-by;
all that my yearning spirit craves is bury me
not in a land of slaves",*

from suffragist Frances Ellen Watkins Harper

"A change is gonna come." ~ Sam Cooke

It felt good to sit and think about how we have had to rise up from where everything started and look to the future at what lies ahead. It made me more excited to head upstairs and see the rest of the museum, especially my grandfather's place in history.

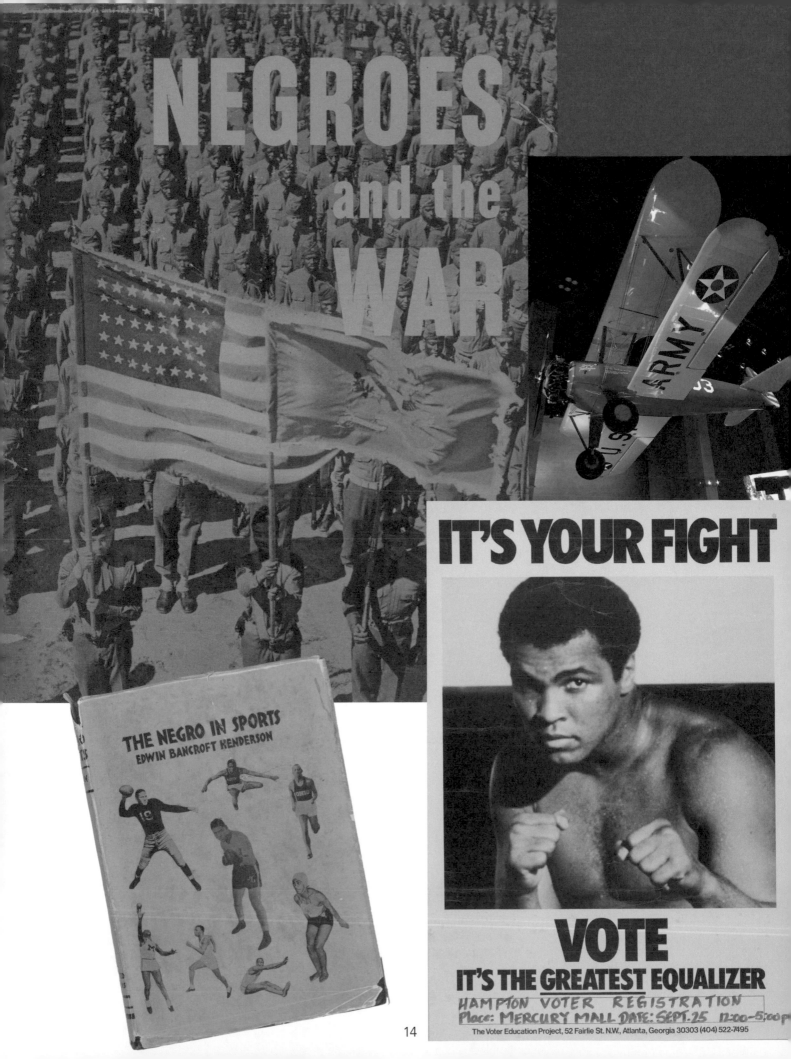

NEGROES and the WAR

IT'S YOUR FIGHT

VOTE
IT'S THE GREATEST EQUALIZER

HAMPTON VOTER REGISTRATION
Place: MERCURY MALL DATE: SEPT. 25 12:00-5:00p
The Voter Education Project, 52 Fairlie St. N.W., Atlanta, Georgia 30303 (404) 522-7495

THE NEGRO IN SPORTS
EDWIN BANCROFT HENDERSON

COMMUNITY GALLERIES
LEVEL 3

Members of The Military

Finally, the chance to see my grandfather's exhibit! This area is packed with so many important African American military heroes, and it was a special moment to see my grandfather's place among them. As the first African American student to attend the Air Force Academy he played an important role in integrating the military academies. His stories told to me were about playing rugby and making life long friends. Spending time at the museum helped me understand that I was spared the uglier details about nastiness from people that did not want him there. Being in this room and seeing so many serviceman that were not just American heroes, but also heroes in the in the African American community by paving the way for equal opportunity and equal treatment for future generations.

Athletes

Wandering through the halls filled with so many statues, memorabilia, and photographs of famous and inspiring athletes is a humbling experience. Learning how many of them had to endure so much racism during the integration of sports, and how much abuse they had to withstand from the public and other players made me grateful for what they did, so that I could have the same opportunity. It is fun to see the statues of great

athletes like Michael Jordan, but there is a more serious side of it too. There is a statue of three Olympic athletes side by side on a podium, gold medalist Tommie Smith, and bronze medalist, John Carlos have their fists raised in defiance, as a symbol of protest at the 1968 Summer Olympics after the 200m race. Threaded throughout the exhibit are instances of how African-American athletes have used their high profile positions and popularity to peacefully protest the unjust and unequal treatment of their people. Whether it's taking a knee, raising a fist, or black armbands, the message is the same. We will stand up for what is right and not stand by and watch people get treated unjustly because of the color of their skin. These athletes chose to use their voice to represent those whose voices weren't being heard, and chose to use their fame to stand up for what was right in the face of a country that didn't want to see it or hear it. When I see football players taking a knee or basketball players wearing a black armband as a form of peaceful protest, **I now understand the history behind it, and that this is not new, in fact it has been happening for generations.**

CULTURE GALLERIES LEVEL 4

Visual Arts and the American Experience

Taking the Stage

African Americans have made great strides in television, film and theatre throughout the years. Fixtures in vaudeville and comedy in nightclubs in the early 1900s, this level follows the gradual integration into television and movies. The offensive black face makeup that was used to mock African Americans by white vaudevillians and then later on in movies, would not end until African Americans were hired more both in front of the camera and behind the camera, when they began to have more control over the story that was being told. Today we have made enormous strides with celebrities like Oprah Winfrey, Tyler Perry and Spike Lee committed to telling stories and providing opportunities both behind the camera and in front of the camera for people of all colors.

Musical Crossroads

Front and center is the king of rock n roll, Chuck Berry's, red Cadillac that he wrote about in many of his songs. Chuck Berry was a big influence on rock n roll, with his unique dancing and guitar skills. Hip hop is represented by Public Enemy which was known for their powerful message of Black pride and strength, and some of their posters and other memorabilia is on display here. The Neighborhood Record Store is an interactive area that lets you pick and choose different types, genres, and generations of music. The importance of African American musicians' influence on all types of music and their important mark they have made on America's musical history is remarkable.

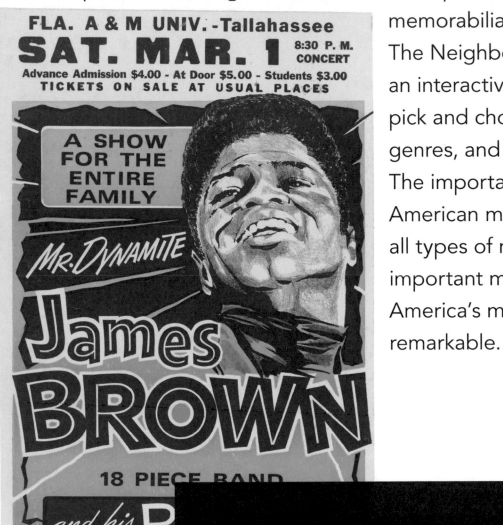

The Green Book

This floor is the most fun because there is so much to do! Best to save it for last! A giant white car in the middle of the floor caught my eye first! When you sit down in it, in front of you is a dashboard that is interactive. Imagine you live in the 1950's and you are driving through the South. **Back then African Americans would not do this without bringing a Green Book.**

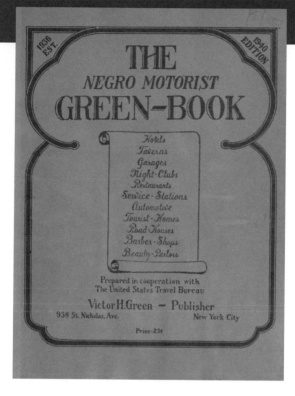

The Green Book was a map used to help them navigate which restaurants, gas stations and hotels were friendly to African Americans and which were not. We got to sit in the car, and pretend we were driving through the South and choose which coffee shop, gas station or hotel to stop at.

A real person would appear on the screen of the dashboard and tell us if we were welcome there, or if we needed to keep moving because they didn't serve "our kind". I wondered if there were still places like this, that did not want to serve you because of the color of your skin but had to anyway because of the law.

The Step Show

My little brother really liked learning how to step with other kids at the interactive step show. We got to learn the African dance steps that are popular in marching bands, fraternities and sororities and have appeared in movies too!

Search for the Sao Jose

The Sao Jose is an 18th century slave ship that sunk, and divers have been searching the wreckage for artifacts. The artifacts will tell us about what it was like on a slave ship during that time. The interactive board lets you search and explore the wreckage.

Robert Frederick Smith Center-
Explore Your Family History

Toward the back of the second floor was a large area, where people could explore their ancestry through the digital database, and also watch videos or listen to oral histories of real people from past generations.

BLACK LIVES MATTERS PROTESTS

At the time of publication, the death of George Floyd by police spurred a wave of protests and marches across the country. Demands for social justice continue to resonate as police shootings of African Americans are gaining notoriety and can no longer be ignored. The BLM civil rights marches of 2020 have included people of all ethnicities, races, and ages as they stand up to join the movement for racial justice. 2020 BLM protests are unique because it is an election year, and we are also suffering from the worst pandemic in our nation's history. **The ongoing civil unrest and protests are sure to find their place in history and in the museum.**

ABOUT THE AUTHORS

The author, **Kyra Bush, is a graduate of UCLA law school and is a member of the California bar.** She earned her bachelor's degree in communications from California State University of Northridge. She is also the mother of four sons.

Kyra is the author of "Why They Kneel", a journey for children and teens about her and her children's walking through the Smithsonian's Natural Museum of African American History.

Kyra donates her time to her children's schools, local San Diego children's organizations, and resource centers.

Christian Sarem is a student, an athlete, and also donates his time to various organizations in the community.

Kyra and her son, Christian, collaborated to write this book not only to serve as a guide to the museum, but also to create, inspire and educate younger generations.

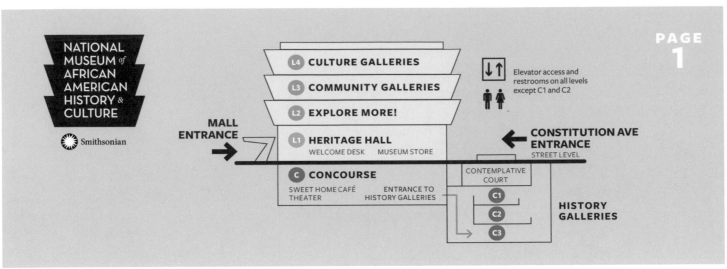

NATIONAL MUSEUM of AFRICAN AMERICAN HISTORY & CULTURE

Smithsonian

L4	CULTURE GALLERIES
L3	COMMUNITY GALLERIES
L2	EXPLORE MORE!
L1	HERITAGE HALL — WELCOME DESK MUSEUM STORE
C	CONCOURSE

MALL ENTRANCE →

CONSTITUTION AVE ENTRANCE — STREET LEVEL

↓↑ 🚹🚺 Elevator access and restrooms on all levels except C1 and C2

CONTEMPLATIVE COURT

C1
C2
C3

SWEET HOME CAFÉ THEATER   ENTRANCE TO HISTORY GALLERIES

HISTORY GALLERIES

L1 HERITAGE HALL

Finding Your Way ▶

CONSTITUTION AVE ENTRANCE ↓

GRAND STAIRCASE

STAIRS ↓↑ ELEVATORS

ESCALATORS

WELCOME DESK

CORONA PAVILION

🚹🚺 LOCKERS

MUSEUM STORE

MALL ENTRANCE ↑

C CONCOURSE

CONTEMPLATIVE COURT

↓↑

EXIT HISTORY GALLERIES

ENTRANCE TO HISTORY GALLERIES

GRAND STAIRCASE

CHANGING EXHIBITION GALLERY

ESCALATORS ↓↑ ELEVATORS
STAIRS

🚹

🚺

OPRAH WINFREY THEATER

SWEET HOME CAFÉ

CAFÉ SEATING

C1 — A CHANGING AMERICA: 1968 AND BEYOND

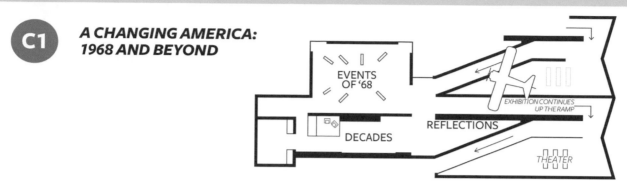

EVENTS OF '68

DECADES

REFLECTIONS

EXHIBITION CONTINUES UP THE RAMP

THEATER

C2 — DEFENDING FREEDOM, DEFINING FREEDOM: THE ERA OF SEGREGATION 1876 – 1968

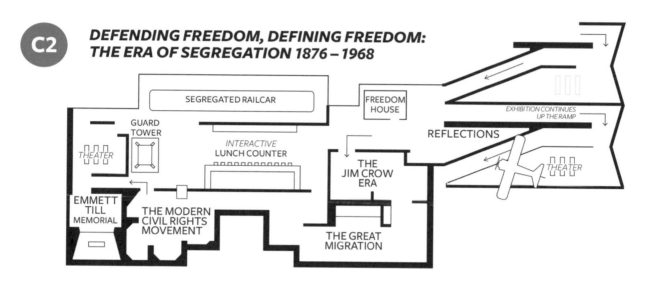

SEGREGATED RAILCAR

FREEDOM HOUSE

EXHIBITION CONTINUES UP THE RAMP

GUARD TOWER

INTERACTIVE LUNCH COUNTER

REFLECTIONS

THEATER

THE JIM CROW ERA

THEATER

EMMETT TILL MEMORIAL

THE MODERN CIVIL RIGHTS MOVEMENT

THE GREAT MIGRATION

C3 — SLAVERY AND FREEDOM 1400 – 1877

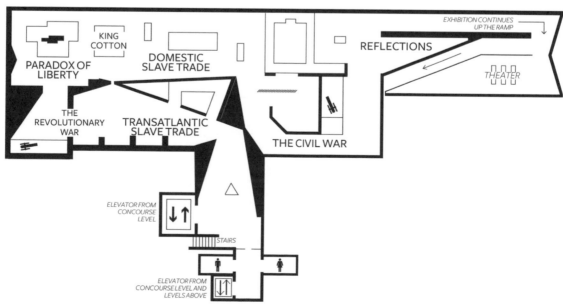

KING COTTON

PARADOX OF LIBERTY

DOMESTIC SLAVE TRADE

REFLECTIONS

EXHIBITION CONTINUES UP THE RAMP

THEATER

THE REVOLUTIONARY WAR

TRANSATLANTIC SLAVE TRADE

THE CIVIL WAR

ELEVATOR FROM CONCOURSE LEVEL

STAIRS

ELEVATOR FROM CONCOURSE LEVEL AND LEVELS ABOVE

L4 CULTURE GALLERIES

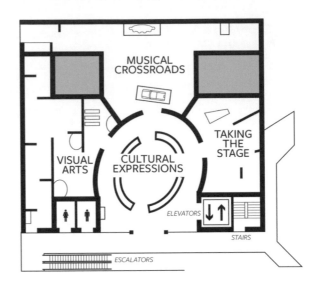

L3 COMMUNITY GALLERIES

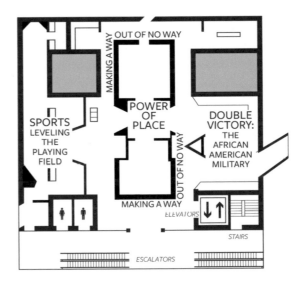

L2 EXPLORE MORE! INTERACTIVE GALLERY

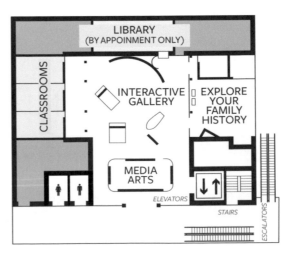

Image Credits

Book Cover:

Diorama of Lunch Counter Sit-Down Protests - National Civil Rights Museum - Downtown Memphis - Tennessee - USA - 01. Adam Jones, Ph.D. Photo credit: Adam Jones, Ph.D./Global Photo Archive/Wikimedia Commons

Mary Church Terrell - Digital ID: (b&w film copy neg.) cph 3b47842 http://hdl.loc.gov/loc.pnp/cph.3b47842. Library of Congress Prints and Photographs Division Washington, D.C. 20540 USA

Created / Published between 1880 and 1900.

Malcolm X - Library of Congress. New York World-Telegram & Sun Collection. http://hdl.loc.gov/loc.pnp/cph.3c15058. Ed Ford, World Telegram staff photographer. PD. "No copyright restriction known. Staff photographer reproduction rights transferred to Library of Congress through Instrument of Gift." Photo credit: NYWT&S staff photo by Ed Ford. Ed Ford—NYWT&S/Library of Congress, Washington, D.C. (LC-USZ62-115058)

Frederick Douglass - Quarter-plate ambrotype of Frederick Douglass. National Portrait Gallery, Smithsonian Institution, Object NPG.74.75. This work is in the public domain in the United States because it was published (or registered with the U.S. Copyright Office) before January 1, 1925.

Kneeling Football Player - iStock

Rosa Parks - Rosa_Parks_being_fingerprinted_by_Deputy_Sheriff_D.H._Lackey_after_being_arrested_on_February_22,_1956,_during_the_Montgomery_bus_boycott.jpg. This work is in the public domain in the United States because it was published in the United States between 1925 and 1977, inclusive, without a copyright notice.

US brig "Perry" and American Slave ship "Martha" off Ambria, June 6th 1850 - https://commons.wikimedia.org/wiki/File:FOOT(1854)_p301_US_BRIG_PERRY_vs._AMERICAN_SLAVE_SHIP_MARTHA_(1850-06-06).jpg . This work is in the public domain in the United States because it was published (or registered with the U.S. Copyright Office) before January 1, 1925.

John Lewis - https://commons.wikimedia.org/wiki/File:John_lewis_official_biopic.jpg. This United States Congress image is in the public domain. This may be because it was taken by an employee of the Congress as part of that person's official duties, or because it has been released into the public domain and posted on the official websites of a member of Congress. As a work of the U.S. federal government, the image is in the public domain.

Jackie Robinson - https://commons.wikimedia.org/wiki/File:Jackie_Robinson,_Brooklyn_Dodgers,_1954.jpg. This is a photo taken by Bob Sandberg when working as a staff photographer of LOOK Magazine, and is part of the LOOK Magazine Photograph Collection at the Library of Congress. Their former owner, Cowles Communications, Inc, dedicated to the public all rights it owned to these images as an instrument of gift. Photo credit: Bob Sandberg, LOOK Magazine.

Charles V. Bush - Photo provided and allowed by Kyra Bush (daughter).

Sewanee Public Desegregation Sign - By Bryanmackinnon - Own work, CC BY-SA 4.0, https://commons.wikimedia.org/w/index.php?curid=36667821. Bryanmackinnon, CC BY-SA 4.0 <https://creativecommons.org/licenses/by-sa/4.0>, via Wikimedia Commons. This file is licensed under the Creative Commons Attribution-Share Alike 4.0 International license. Photo credit: Bryan Mackinnon

Muhammad Ali - https://commons.wikimedia.org/wiki/File:Muhammad_Ali_NYWTS.jpg. Ira Rosenberg, Public domain, via Wikimedia Commons. This image is available from the United States Library of Congress's Prints and Photographs division under the digital ID cph.3c15435. This work is from the New York World-Telegram and Sun collection at the Library of Congress. According to the library, there are no known copyright restrictions on the use of this work. https://www.loc.gov/pictures/item/96500238/. This photograph is a work for hire created prior to 1968 by a staff photographer at New York World-Telegram & Sun. It is part of a collection donated to the Library of Congress and per the instrument of gift it is in the public domain. Photo credit: Ira Rosenberg,1916-2016, New York World-Telegram and Sun collection.

Dr. Martin Luther King, Jr. - Civil_Rights_March_on_Washington,_D.C._(Dr._Martin_Luther_King,_Jr._and_Mathew_Ahmann_in_a_crowd.)_-_NARA_-_542015_-_Restoration.jpg. This media is available in the holdings of the National Archives and Records Administration, cataloged under the National Archives Identifier (NAID). No known copyright restriction. https://catalog.archives.gov/id/542015. Photo credit: Rowland Scherman.

Harriet Tubman - https://commons.wikimedia.org/wiki/File:Harriet_Tubman.tif. This work is in the public domain in the United States because it was published (or registered with the U.S. Copyright Office) before January 1, 1925. Illustration by J.C. Darby (1865).

National Museum of African American History & Culture / Smithsonian - Photo credit: Alan Karchmer/NMAAHC.

Interior Images:

INTRODUCTION

Raised fist statue. Provided and allowed by Kyra Bush

PROLOGUE

Images of Kyra and children at exhibits (3) - Provided and allowed by Kyra Bush.

HISTORY GALLERIES

Slave Ship - https://commons.wikimedia.org/wiki/File:FOOT(1854)_p301_US_BRIG_PERRY_vs._AMERICAN_SLAVE_SHIP_MARTHA_(1850-06-06).jpg. This work is in the public domain in the United States because it was published (or registered with the U.S. Copyright Office) before January 1, 1925.

Collection box of the Rhode Island Anti-Slavery Society owned by Garrison family 1830s - 1850s - 2014.115.9. Created by: Rhode Island Anti-Slavery Society. Owned by: George Thompson Garrison. Collection of the Smithsonian National Museum of African American History and Culture, Gift of the Garrison Family in memory of George Thompson Garrison

C2-DEFENDING FREEDOM

Rosa Parks - Rosa_Parks_being_fingerprinted_by_Deputy_Sheriff_D.H._Lackey_after_being_arrested_on_February_22,_1956,_during_the_Montgomery_bus_boycott.jpg. This work is in the public domain in the United States because it was published in the United States between 1925 and 1977, inclusive, without a copyright notice.

MODERN CIVIL RIGHT MOVEMENT

Dr. Martin Luther King, Jr. - Civil_Rights_March_on_Washington,_D.C._(Dr._Martin_Luther_King,_Jr._and_Mathew_Ahmann_in_a_crowd.)_-_NARA_-_542015_-_Restoration.jpg. This media is available in the holdings of the National Archives and Records Administration, cataloged under the National Archives Identifier (NAID). No known copyright restriction. https://catalog.archives.gov/id/542015. Photo credit: Rowland Scherman. Restoration.jpg. This media is available in the holdings of the National Archives and Records Administration, cataloged under the National Archives Identifier (NAID). Scherman, Rowland, Photographer. https://catalog.archives.gov/id/542015

DECADES

Placard for 2008 Obama presidential campaign 2008 - Created by: MoveOn.org. Subject of: President Barack Obama. Collection of the Smithsonian National Museum of African American History and Culture.

WATERFALL-CONCOURSE

Waterfall - Photo credit: Alan Karchmer/NMAAHC

Smaller Waterfall - Provided and allowed by Kyra Bush.

COMMUNITY GALLERIES: MILITARY / ATHLETES

Negroes and the War - Published by: United States Office of War Information. Photograph by: Eliot Elisofon. Written by: Chandler Owen. 1942. Collection of the Smithsonian National Museum of African American History and Culture, in Memory of Eliot Elisofon

Tuskegee Airmen Biplane - Provided and allowed by Kyra Bush.

The Negro in Sports - Written by: Edwin Bancroft Henderson. Published by: The Associated Publishers, Inc. 1939. Collection of the Smithsonian National Museum of African American History and Culture.

Poster for voting rights featuring Muhammad Ali - Created by: Voter Education Project. Subject of: Muhammad Ali. 1960s. Collection of the Smithsonian National Museum of African American History and Culture.

Christian posing next to Michael Jordan statue - Provided and allowed by Kyra Bush.

CULTURE GALLERIES

Poster for Harlem on the Prairie - Created by: Toddy Pictures Company. Subject of: Herb Jeffries. Subject of: Consuela Harris. Subject of: Mantan Moreland. Subject of: Flournoy Miller. 1937. Collection of the Smithsonian National Museum of African American History and Culture

Poster advertising a James Brown concert at Florida A&M University - Printed by: Globe Poster Printing Company. Subject of: James Brown. Subject of: Florida A&M University. 1969. Collection of the Smithsonian National Museum of African American History and Culture.

Red Cadillac Eldorado owned by Chuck Berry - Created by: General Motors Corporation. Owned by: Chuck Berry. 1973. Collection of the Smithsonian National Museum of African American History and Culture.

EXPLORE MORE! INTERACTIVE AREA

The Negro Motorist Green Book - (1940 edition) by Victor Hugo Green. https://commons.wikimedia.org/wiki/File:The_Negro_Motorist_Green_Book.jpg The depicted text is ineligible for copyright and therefore in the public domain, because it is not a "literary work" or other protected type in sense of the local copyright law. Facts, data, and unoriginal information which is common property without sufficiently creative authorship in a general typeface or basic handwriting, and simple geometric shapes are not protected by copyright.

The Step Show - Provided and allowed by Kyra Bush.

BLACK LIVES MATTER PROTESTS

George Floyd Mural - https://commons.wikimedia.org/wiki/File:George_Floyd_mural_Mauerpark_Berlin_2020-05-30_02.jpg. I, the copyright holder of this work, hereby publish it under the following license:

This file is made available under the Creative Commons CC0 1.0 Universal Public Domain Dedication.

The person who associated a work with this deed has dedicated the work to the public domain by waiving all of their rights to the work worldwide under copyright law, including all related and neighboring rights, to the extent allowed by law. You can copy, modify, distribute and perform the work, even for commercial purposes, all without asking permission. The photographical reproduction of this work is covered under the article § 59 of the German copyright law, which states that "It shall be permissible to reproduce, by painting, drawing, photography or cinematography, works which are permanently located on public ways, streets or places and to distribute and publicly communicate such copies. For works of architecture, this provision shall be applicable only to the external appearance." As with all other "limits of copyright by legally permitted uses", no changes to the actual work are permitted under § 62 of the German copyright law (UrhG). ~Leonhard Lenz

ABOUT THE AUTHORS

Kyra Bush & Christian Sarem - Provided and allowed by Kyra Bush.

Printed in the United States
by Baker & Taylor Publisher Services